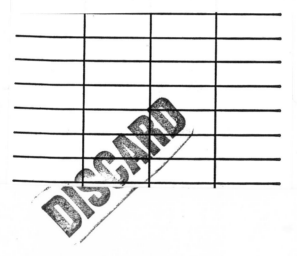

# SCIENCE TO THE RESCUE
## ADAPTING TO CLIMATE CHANGE™

# ADAPTING TO INTENSE STORMS

ADAM FURGANG

*For Kathy*

Published in 2013 by The Rosen Publishing Group, Inc.
29 East 21st Street, New York, NY 10010

## Library of Congress Cataloging-in-Publication Data

Furgang, Adam.
Adapting to intense storms/Adam Furgang.—1st ed.
    p. cm.—(Science to the rescue: adapting to climate change)
Includes bibliographical references and index.
ISBN 978-1-4488-6848-3 (library binding)
1. Storms—Juvenile literature. 2. Climatic changes—Juvenile literature. 3. Climatic extremes—Juvenile literature. 4. Weather forecasting—Juvenile literature. I. Title.
QC941.3.F87 2013
551.55—dc23

                               2011047779

*Manufactured in the United States of America*

CPSIA Compliance Information: Batch #S12YA: For further information, contact Rosen Publishing, New York, New York, at 1-800-237-9932.

# CONtents

# INTROduction

On Sunday, May 22, 2011, a little over an hour and a half after Dr. Kevin Kikta started his shift as an emergency room doctor at St. John's Regional Medical Hospital in Joplin, Missouri, the unthinkable happened. A powerful tornado ripped through the town. The following is his personal account, told to a reporter for the television station KMOV, of what happened just after he took shelter under a desk:

> We heard a loud horrifying sound, like a large locomotive ripping through the hospital. The whole hospital shook and vibrated as we heard glass shattering, lightbulbs popping, walls collapsing, people screaming, the ceiling caving in above us, and water pipes breaking, showering water down on everything. We suffered this in complete darkness, unaware of anyone else's status, worried, scared. We could feel a tight pressure in our heads as the tornado annihilated the hospital and the surrounding

Rescue workers search the remains of a destroyed house in the wake of a killer hurricane.

area. The whole process took about forty-five seconds, but seemed like eternity. The hospital had just taken a direct hit from a category EF-4 tornado.

Then it was over. Just forty-five seconds. Forty-five long seconds. We looked at each other, terrified, and thanked God that we were alive. We didn't know, but hoped that it was safe enough to go back out to the ED [Emergency Department], find the rest of the staff and patients, and assess our losses.

Like a bomb went off. That's the only way that I can describe what we saw next. Patients were coming into the ED in droves. It was absolute, utter chaos. They were limping, bleeding, crying, terrified, with debris and glass sticking out of them, just thankful to be alive.

The tornado that hit Joplin, Missouri, was the single deadliest tornado in U.S. history, with about 151 people killed. The storm came just weeks after an incredibly stormy April—the most active tornado month on record. According to the National Oceanic and Atmospheric Administration (NOAA), April 2011 saw 875 tornadoes, with 361 fatalities.

Severe and deadly storms like the one in Joplin seem to have become both more frequent and more intense in recent years. The frequency and severity of tornadoes, hurricanes, tropical storms, thunderstorms, blizzards, ice storms, dust storms, and cyclones have all increased around the globe. Scientists tell us that this developing trend will only become worse. They have found evidence that these storms are likely triggered by an overall warming of the planet, due largely to human activity, particularly the burning of heat-trapping fossil fuels.

This phenomenon is known as climate change, or global warming. The very conditions that trigger typical weather events—warming ocean waters and a warming atmosphere—have increased around the globe. As a result, we will almost certainly be hit with more frequent and more damaging, even catastrophic, storms.

Living with these killer storms can be challenging, but humans are learning to adapt to changing climatic situations. Technology allows us to design and build stronger homes than ever before. We can predict weather faster and with more precision. We are able to communicate this important information more quickly and over more media and platforms (television, radio, e-mail and smartphone alerts, etc.) than ever before, enabling people to get to safety before storms strike. We can even react faster than ever to tragedies and rescue and care for people in dire need after a deadly storm strikes an area.

# CHAPTER one

# Assessing the Problem

In order to explain the emerging trend of more frequent and more intense storms, one must look at the causes of global warming and climate change. Scientists have provided evidence that human activities are causing a buildup of heat-trapping gases in the atmosphere. Data collected worldwide has shown an overall increase in global surface temperatures. The overall increase has been about 1 degree Fahrenheit (0.55 degree Celsius) over the past one hundred years or so. This may sound insignificant, but even this small average increase is enough to produce a noticeable effect on weather events, which occur due to atmospheric conditions such as temperature.

## INDUSTRIALIZATION AND WARMING

The increase in global surface temperatures began at the same time that the Industrial Revolution was getting underway. The rise has been in direct proportion to the increase in industrialized activities, which are heavily dependent upon the burning of fossil fuels. At the start of the Industrial Revolution, at the end of the eighteenth century, nations such as Great Britain and the United States began using machinery to get work done. They relied more and more heavily on machines in the years that followed. This included steam power for trains, factories that manufactured goods, and the mass production of goods for an ever-increasing population.

Powering the Industrial Age required doing something that hadn't been done before often—burning fossil fuels, such as coal, oil, and gas. In order to get factories and machines to run, lots of power had to be generated. The burning of coal was one way to provide the energy needed to make factories run, heat homes and businesses, and provide electrical power to large numbers of people.

When cars began to be manufactured on assembly lines in the United States, people all over the country were suddenly able to buy them at more affordable prices. All of those cars needed gasoline to make them run. As a result, more fossil fuels were extracted from the ground, refined into petroleum, and burned in large quantities in the cars'

Steam engines like this one ran on fossil fuels and contributed to the production of pollution and greenhouse gases throughout much of the twentieth century.

combustion engines. When fossil fuels are burned to power factories and provide heat and electricity to homes, pollution escapes into the air. Similarly, when a car consumes gasoline, fumes are released into the air from the exhaust pipe.

Despite greater research on and knowledge about the greenhouse phenomenon, by the turn of the twenty-first century, fossil-fuel burning and the resulting carbon-based, heat-trapping emissions were only increasing. Today, many North American families have more than one car. Automobile use is becoming common even in underdeveloped countries where cars were once rare luxury goods.

The release of greenhouse gases, specifically carbon dioxide, into the atmosphere is the crux of the problem that causes climate change. Carbon dioxide by itself is not a dangerous gas. In fact, you breathe it out with every exhalation of breath.

Plants require carbon dioxide for respiration, and humans require the oxygen produced by plants as an end product of this process. The components that make up greenhouse gases on Earth are water vapor, carbon dioxide, methane, and ozone.

A phenomenon known as the greenhouse effect occurs when the sun's heat becomes trapped in the lower portion of the atmosphere near Earth's surface. This effect is an ordinarily beneficial phenomenon that keeps Earth's atmosphere from losing too much of the sun's heat and becoming too cold to support life. But the additional greenhouse gases that humans produce become trapped in the atmosphere and cause an over-all rise in temperatures. It's the massive increase in the production and accumulation of carbon dioxide due to industrialization that is leading to rising temperatures and climate change.

## BANDING TOGETHER

Since 1992, environmental and political leaders have been trying to decrease the greenhouse gases in the atmosphere. The Earth Summit in Rio de Janeiro and the UN Framework Convention on Climate Change (both in 1992) were both important efforts to get leaders of various countries to agree to limit their nations' greenhouse gas emissions. Since then, several nations have voluntarily reduced their emissions of the most dangerous greenhouse gases: carbon dioxide, methane, nitrous oxide, and sulfur hexafluoride.

In January of 2010, the United States pledged to reduce its greenhouse gas emissions by 17 percent by 2020. Individual states are also doing their part. The 2009 Regional Greenhouse Gas Initiative included ten East Coast states that had voluntarily agreed to cap their greenhouse gas emissions. The states are Connecticut, Delaware, Maine, Maryland, Massachusetts, New Hampshire, New Jersey, New York, Rhode Island, and Vermont.

In order to understand how weather patterns and events are being disrupted and intensified by climate change and global warming, we must first start by examining what have been considered typical weather patterns. Then the extent and nature of climate change–driven deviations from these norms may become clearer.

# THE NATIONAL CLIMATE ASSESSMENT

In 1990, the U.S. Global Change Research Act was passed. This law requires that a climate change report be delivered to the president and Congress periodically. The report evaluates the most recent climate data, gathered with the help of the latest technologies, and then compares this new data to existing climate change models. There are thirteen agencies that cooperate and pool their research for these studies. The National Climate Assessment's most recent report stated that there are noticeable climate change–related phenomena occurring in the United States and the oceans surrounding it. The study revealed an increase in average precipitation, rising sea levels and temperatures, and river flow alterations—all sure signs of warming and climate change.

# THUNDERSTORMS

Everyone has experienced thunderstorms. They are the most common form of severe weather. Thunderstorms occur when warm, moist air rises quickly. When this water vapor meets the cooler air above it, the vapor cools and condenses, forming clouds. Some of these clouds reach very high altitudes, and then water droplets fall as rain. Storms can often be accompanied by electrostatic discharges from clouds, called lightning. When the static discharge occurs, the surrounding air is heated quickly and intensely, causing

Thunderstorms are the most common form of severe weather. Damaging lightning is caused by electrostatic discharges from clouds.

the air to expand rapidly. This expansion of air as the result of lightning is called thunder.

Thunderstorms most often occur in the afternoon, after the air has been heated all day. Some thunderstorms produce the type of cloud that could develop into a tornado. An increase in the overall temperature of Earth's atmosphere will cause thunderstorms to form more frequently, and the damage done by the storms would be more apparent and more costly.

## TORNADOES

Tornadoes form most often in spring and summer, when the ground becomes warmer and the air above it is cooler. A tornado may form during a thunderstorm, when warm winds near the ground blow in one direction and cool air aloft blows in the opposite direction. The two masses of air begin to rotate. The warm, rising air that causes the thunderstorm pulls the rotating air mass so that it forms a vortex. This rotating air may cause a tornado if a funnel cloud connects the vortex to the ground.

Tornadoes can have wind speeds of more than 260 miles per hour (418 kilometers per hour) and can suck many objects into their path. Most tornadoes last just a few minutes and are a few hundred yards wide. A tornado destroys most things in its path, yet it can leave homes or other objects beyond its reach completely untouched.

Tornadoes may occur anywhere, but some areas are more prone to this destructive weather phenomenon than others. The Great Plains area in the central United States is

Tornadoes like this one can be extremely damaging to property and can cause many deaths. They can form quickly and touch down with very little warning.

known as Tornado Alley. Warm air coming in from the Gulf of Mexico in the springtime meets up with cold, dry air from Canada and the Rocky Mountains, causing the conditions that are just right for tornadoes to form. According to predictive models, an increase in ocean temperatures would encourage conditions favorable to tornado formation and increase their power. Even with the as yet small increase in ocean temperatures to date, the frequency of tornadoes does indeed seem to have increased.

# HURRICANES

Hurricanes start out as tropical storms that begin over warm ocean waters. The warming waters of the North Atlantic, the Gulf of Mexico, the Caribbean Sea, or the Northeast Pacific Ocean can cause what's generally known as a hurricane. Depending on their location, hurricanes can go by other names. They are called typhoons in the Northwest Pacific Ocean. In the Indian Ocean and near the ocean waters of Australia, they are called cyclones.

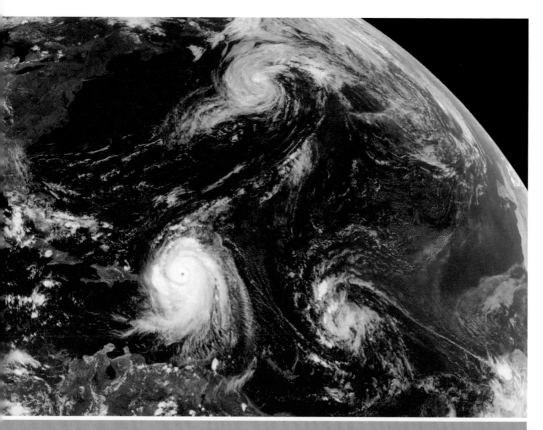

Tropical storms form over warm ocean waters. They may gain strength and be classified as a hurricane before making landfall. Hurricanes have wind speeds from 74 to155 miles per hour (119 to 249 km/hr).

No matter what their name, tropical storms occur when warm air at the surface of the ocean rises quickly. This rising air will soon meet up with cooler air above it, and the rising water vapor will cool and condense into storm clouds. As the clouds condense, heat is released, warming the air above the clouds. In turn, the clouds rise higher, making more room for humid air below the clouds.

The storm is being slowly fed with moist air. The exchange of heat from the surface of the ocean to the atmosphere and back down again makes wind appear in a swirling pattern. The swirling pattern around the classic eye of the storm forms when winds near the surface of the ocean push together and water vapor is pushed upward, contributing further to the already circulating warm air. When the winds become greater than 74 miles per hour (119 km/hr), the storm is upgraded from a tropical storm and is classified as a hurricane.

By the time hurricanes and tropical storms reach land, the winds have pushed the ocean water to well above normal levels. This temporary increase in sea level is called a storm surge. Some storm surges can be up to 25 to 30 feet (8 to 9 meters), causing massive flooding when they reach land. Hurricane winds are also extremely damaging. The strongest hurricanes can have wind speeds over 155 miles per hour (249 km/hr), which is enough to destroy homes and create deadly flying debris.

Because they derive their energy from warm ocean waters, hurricanes and tropical storms tend to lose their strength as they move inland. Yet the heavy rains that even downgraded hurricanes produce can cause massive flooding of rivers.

With the increased air temperatures associated with global warming, hurricanes form more frequently. In addition, the warmer air over the oceans can cause the hurricanes to increase in strength and wind speed, causing even greater damage when they finally make landfall.

Blizzards can leave huge snowbanks for months, like the one shown here in Oswego, New York.

## BLIZZARDS

Similar to a thunderstorm, a blizzard is caused when high and low pressure systems collide. Because the air is typically so cold in winter, however, the resulting precipitation is snow instead of rain. Blizzards have winds of at least 35 miles per hour (56 km/hr), causing little to no visibility because of the blowing snow. Blizzards can bring several feet of snow, take out power lines, and create icy and whiteout conditions that are dangerous to drive in.

Some people have questioned whether or not an increase in winter weather events such as blizzards is a sign of climate change and global warming. Some people feel that an increase in snowstorms would seem to argue against global warming. However, an increase in all weather events—whether winter blizzards or summer tropical storms—would be consistent with the predictions of climate scientists. These researchers foresee an increase in precipitation and storminess for certain parts of the world due to a chain of factors that result from increasing air and ocean temperatures.

Humans are already beginning to deal with more frequent and intense storms that are likely directly related to global warming. This is not something that only those in the tropics are suffering. North Americans are increasingly experiencing the destabilizing effects of warming temperatures and the violent and catastrophic storms they can produce. For example, in February 2007, consecutive blizzards in Oswego, New York, left the area with 11 feet (3 m) of snow. People were stranded in their homes, cars, shopping malls, and airports, and left without power for weeks.

# CHAPTER two

# Predictions of a Changing Climate

Scientific records have allowed us to keep track of how the climate has changed over the past century, but we must now look ahead to predict how such changes will likely continue in the future. This involves developing technologies and climate models that can accurately predict the effects of climate change.

## MODELING THE FUTURE

Since the 1950s, mathematical models have been able to represent seasonal patterns in the atmosphere. In the 1960s, computers were able to precisely chart the circulation of air over water and land. They were also able to account for increasing carbon-based emissions into the atmosphere, resulting in far more accurate climate models. By the 1980s, computer models were able to focus on specific areas of the globe, and the National Center for Atmospheric Research has been continuing to improve this technology.

Today, computer climate models can be quite complex. Although scientists state that mean temperatures around the world are increasing, a close look at the models shows that there are some areas of the world that have been

This weather station is located in a shipping container in Canada and is used to study cloud formations above the Arctic. The data is used to help understand climate change.

experiencing decreasing surface temperatures. These kinds of local variations and discrepancies can make climate data confusing and difficult to explain. A poor understanding of the climate models and global climate patterns also allows climate-change skeptics to exploit the potential confusion and spread the message that there is no cause for alarm.

The data that the climate models are based on has been collected through the cooperation of eighty-five countries. The United Nations World Meteorological Organization (WMO) coordinates more than ten thousand manned and automatic surface weather stations, one thousand upper-air stations, over seven thousand ships, more than one hundred moored and one thousand drifting buoys, hundreds of weather radars, and over three thousand specially equipped commercial aircraft that measure key parameters of the atmosphere, land, and ocean surface every day. In addition, the WMO Observing System contains operational polar-orbiting and geostationary satellites and research and development environmental satellites that complement the ground-based global observations.

## RISING TEMPERATURES

Based on the data continuously gathered by these stations, today's computer climate models are now able to predict how temperatures will change over the next decades and into the next century. The models can be adjusted to show what would happen if various greenhouse gases in the atmosphere decreased, increased, or remained the same. For example, one scenario may assume a 3 percent annual

# WHAT COULD HAPPEN?

If the overall temperatures on Earth increased up to 3°F (1.7°C), as some models suggest is likely, what would that mean for people living in North America? Here are the implications of such increases:

- An increase of 1°F (0.6°C): Droughts would be very common throughout the western United States, which could become more desertlike. These areas have already been experiencing record-high temperatures well over 100°F (38°C) during the summer. The agriculture and crops that we rely on in these areas would be impossible to maintain in the changed climate.

- An increase of 2°F (1.1°C): Areas in Canada and the United States that rely on mountain runoff for water supplies will have a sharp shortage of water. The amount of snow melting off mountains could decrease by up to 70 percent. Winter snows would melt much quicker and flow into rivers during the winter instead of well into the spring and summer months.

- An increase of 3°F (1.7°C): In addition to difficult wildfires and heat waves, coastal areas all along the North American East Coast will have increased ocean levels due to the melting of ice sheets near the North Pole.

decrease in greenhouse gas emissions beginning in 2010. Even when this hypothetical decrease is input into the computer model, the world's average overall temperature is still projected to increase another 3 to 10°F (2 to 6°C) by the year 2100. That's a much faster increase than we saw in the last century. The models have provided scientists with valuable information about climate change, what contributes to it, and what its consequences are.

Take for example, an increase of 5°F (3°C). With such an increase, many places that are already considered warm climates would no longer be able to sustain life. Many species of plants and animals would become extinct. The increased temperatures would cause more frequent deadly storms and severe droughts, as well as a rise in sea levels when glaciers in the Northern Hemisphere melt away into the ocean. Flooding would affect our ability to grow and harvest food. Areas that are not used to certain types of severe weather will have to deal with their consequences. Tornadoes all around the world will be more common, and hurricanes outside of warm, tropical areas will also occur more frequently. All of this could lead to human suffering and death, food and water shortages, and mass migrations.

## AN ONGOING DEBATE

Many scientists agree that global warming and climate change are both real and observable phenomena, and they are well underway. The effects of warming and climate change are already being felt, and they are almost certainly irreversible in the short term. Climate scientists have tried—with varying degrees of success—to use the data and models to persuade political leaders to make and enforce laws that would mandate sharp reductions in emissions of carbon-based, heat-trapping gases. However, despite all of the data-gathering and computer-driven calculations, the models are just that—models. They are not hard facts or sure-fire certainties. There has been an increasing debate over the accuracy of the models and of their ability to predict real climate change.

Even though climate models can change based upon newly gathered data and shifting variables, the general trends in the predictions have remained fairly constant and are agreed upon by most scientists in the field. The current levels of greenhouses gases trapped in the atmosphere will remain there for a long time, with carbon dioxide, in particular, lingering for hundreds of years even if no more is added from this point forward. This is why reversing the effects of global warming is highly unlikely in the short term, even with drastic emission-cutting measures. Most climate models paint a similar picture—more warming will occur at the poles and in northern areas, and many areas would be left uninhabitable, requiring mass relocations of millions of people. Yet global warming experts have been met with skepticism and controversy ever since they began releasing the results of their climate models.

The issue of global warming has become a political issue. The scientific data implies that a drastic change has to be made in public policy, corporate practice, industrial activity, and consumer habits. In short, we have to radically alter the way we live, work, travel, and consume. Anyone who

Some scientists and global warming skeptics feel that climate change data is inaccurate because it cannot consider all factors, such as the overall cooling effects that unexpected volcanic eruptions could have on the climate.

suggests that we must drastically change how we live our lives, what we drive, and how we run our businesses is bound to be met with scrutiny. They will be challenged by critics and those who stand to lose money as new energy sources, consumer habits, and corporate practices are explored and adopted. Such changes are costly and can cause considerable economic and social disruptions and dislocations.

Another reason climate change skeptics do not like the current prediction models is that they do not account for some events, such as volcanic eruptions, which have an overall cooling effect on the climate. Some people think that unknown variables such as this make the data inaccurate and our climatic future uncertain and unknowable.

Regardless of the way individual climate studies are interpreted or the political maneuvering that drives competing claims regarding global warming, a large number of people—including the vast majority of climate scientists—agree that the climate does seem to be changing. There are more frequent and intense storms and weather events. There are more floods and droughts worldwide, they are occurring more often, and they are more severe. Given these widely held, research-supported assumptions, the question is: how do humans adapt to the effects of climate change—such as an increase in the frequency and intensity of storms? And how do we guarantee our long-term survival as a race?

# CHAPTER three

# Adapting to Today's Changing Climate

There is still debate about whether humans are responsible for the increase of greenhouse gases building up in the atmosphere. Yet there is little dispute about the fact that global surface temperatures are rising and that climate around the world is in the process of changing. One result of these developments is a corresponding increase in the frequency and intensity of storms. As a result, no matter what is causing the changes to our climate, humans are forced to improve storm preparedness, storm alert systems, building codes, and procedures for first responders and emergency management teams.

## STORM FORECASTING

Forecasting the weather has become a much more precise science than in decades past. Meteorologists still cannot predict every twist and turn in the weather, but modern satellite systems and radar help spot storms forming thousands

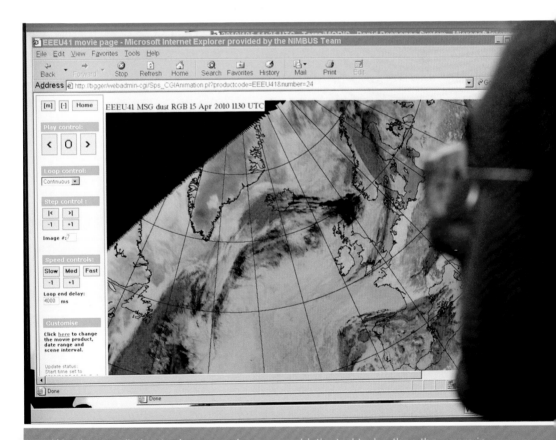

Weather prediction tools are much more sophisticated today than they were in the past. This satellite image shows a huge volcanic ash plume moving toward England, the result of the eruption of a volcano in Iceland.

of miles out to sea. They can then track each storm's development and movements and warn people in the path of it to be prepared.

Because of these advances in weather prediction and tracking, communicating storm-related news and warnings has become much better in recent years. Now news stations provide alerts and warnings in enough time for people to prepare for coming storms. People can look on the Internet to find satellite maps showing where a storm is currently located and where its path is predicted to be in the next several days or even hours. Being prepared for the intense storms that will likely become more common with global warming is an important way for humans to adapt to the problem. When they see a strong and destructive storm coming, they can get out of the way of the destruction well ahead of time.

## STORM PREPAREDNESS

When people are warned of storms well ahead of time, they can take the necessary precautions to protect their homes from damage. They can also remove themselves from harm's way and possibly avoid injury or even death. Especially in coastal areas that are hit with frequent hurricanes, storm preparedness is an important way to adapt to a changing environment that encourages stronger and more frequent weather events.

To protect homes and businesses from winds above 100 miles per hour (161 km/hr), simple precautions can be taken, such as nailing boards over windows to keep them from shattering in high winds and possibly causing harm to those inside. Even taping the windows will keep the glass from shattering as badly as it would if left unprotected. Bringing in any loose and unsecured objects from a property—such as toys, bikes, lawn furniture, and grills—can minimize damage to property, prevent injuries, and save lives. Excessive winds can pick up even heavy objects, carrying them long distances and wreaking havoc when they come crashing back to the ground.

The Saffir-Simpson Hurricane Wind Scale rates hurricanes based on their potential to do harm to people and property. For example, a Category 1 hurricane with wind speeds from 74 to 95 miles per hour (119 to 153 km/hr)—the least powerful type of hurricane—can create falling or flying debris that puts people, pets, and livestock at risk of injury and death. Mobile homes can experience damage to their roofing shingles and siding, even if they are anchored to the ground properly. Permanent homes may suffer damage to shingles, gutters, and chimneys.

A Category 5 hurricane can cause major damage. With winds in excess of 155 miles per hour (249 km/hr), catastrophic damage can occur. People, pets, and livestock run a very high risk of injury or death from flying debris, even if they remain indoors. Mobile homes may be completely destroyed, regardless of how well they are built. A high percentage of permanent frame homes can be destroyed, with total failure of many roofs and walls. Power outages may last for weeks or even months, and water shortages are possible.

While we may not be able to eliminate the damage caused by Category 5 hurricanes, it helps to understand the destructive potential the storms have and prepare for them as much as possible. With our current meteorological, computer modeling, and predictive technologies, we already know a lot about the behavior of hurricanes as they hit land. This information at our disposal includes a hurricane's wind speeds, its category rating on the Saffir-Simpson scale, and its approximate arrival time on land and likely path. Preparing for storms with this kind of potential for damage is important for saving both property and lives. Today's meteorological and communication technologies give people in the path of the storm several days to prepare for the worst and/or evacuate from the area if needed or ordered to do so.

## RETHINKING ZONING LAWS

For decades, people have rebuilt in the wake of storms that have devastated their homes, even when those locations were obviously vulnerable to storm damage. With the increasing frequency and ferocity of storms, this kind of stubborn rebuilding activity is being reconsidered. When certain areas are repeatedly hit by destructive storms, it seems increasingly prudent to avoid development there.

In August of 2011, Hurricane Irene traveled up the East Coast of the United States. As it traveled north of New York City, it was downgraded to a tropical storm. Yet even in its weakened state, the storm caused devastating flooding in parts of New Jersey, upstate New York, and Vermont. Some areas within the Catskill Mountains were nearly washed away

Tropical Storm Irene caused severe flooding of New Jersey's Passaic River. This flooding was rare, but some areas seem to be affected by storms over and over again. In those situations, governments may reconsider allowing land to be developed in known flood zones.

by overflowing creeks. This was not the first time such flooding occurred in the Catskills. In 1996 and again in 2005, the same areas had flooded severely. The question of whether or not to rebuild homes and businesses in this part of the Catskills is a serious consideration. Many officials and politicians believe it is time to reconsider building codes and rebuilding policies in flood zones.

The so-called Great Flood of 1993 also prompted a similar reappraisal of development and rebuilding policies in flood-prone areas. Increased rainfall during the fall of 1993 caused the Missouri and Upper Mississippi rivers to overflow. The flood covered 400,00 square miles (1,035,995 sq km) over nine states and lasted almost two hundred days. There were important lessons learned from this flood. Instead of rebuilding on the land, the government decided to buy out many homes so that people would not be able to build in the flood zone again. The flooded areas were then turned into parks and wildlife habitats. Entire communities were moved, such as the town of Valmeyer, Illinois. The town was rebuilt 2 miles (3 km) away and 400 feet (122 m) above the floodplain of the Mississippi River.

With an increasing number of storms expected in upcoming years, the idea of building or rebuilding in floodplains is one that needs to be deliberated carefully. More caution is now being shown when considering where communities should be placed so that citizens' lives and properties are not put directly in the path of danger.

# INTERNATIONAL SAFETY STANDARDS

There are now efforts underway to make buildings all around the world as safe as possible. The International Code Council is trying to get a set of international building codes adopted by most countries. Poverty is a big factor in how strict or lax building codes are. Generally, the poorer the country, the weaker its building codes and buildings. Countries with little funds may end up with inferior and unsafe buildings. It is a difficult effort to get these codes drafted, instituted, and enforced worldwide. But the effort is necessary so that lives can be kept as safe as possible in the face of climate change and the increasingly frequent and destructive storms it fosters.

# DISASTER RESPONSE

With each major storm, authorities learn how to handle destructive weather events better and better. The lessons learned from Hurricane Katrina in 2005 have caused many changes in the way governments both prepare for and respond to looming storms. Warnings are put into place as soon as possible, and evacuations are ordered and supervised in as orderly a manner as possible.

Governments tend to be cautious when considering evacuations. They know that an evacuation may be inconvenient, but it helps to minimize deaths and injuries and post-storm rescue missions. Each storm that must be dealt with is serious, with evacuation considerations to be made about the elderly, the sick, and those residing in especially vulnerable areas. A plan must be put in place for how to organize and carry out large-scale evacuations and where to shelter those who must flee their homes.

The job of first responders after destructive weather events is crucial to the saving of lives; the sheltering, clothing, and feeding of the displaced; and the cleanup of storm-ravaged areas. When local and state authorities cannot handle the cleanup from storm damages, other agencies get involved. The Federal Emergency Management Agency (FEMA) sets up shelters and assists people who have lost their homes to storm damage or flooding. The American Red Cross, which started in 1881, is a disaster response agency that has grown so large that it now responds to over sixty-seven thousand disasters each year. It has more than seven hundred local

An Alabama woman talks with a FEMA agent after her home was destroyed by a tornado.

branches and over a half million volunteers. They provide food, blankets, clothes, and other supplies that people who have been displaced by storms desperately need. Red Cross volunteers are trained to deal with the results of severe storms, including rescuing stranded storm victims; feeding and clothing them; and providing first aid, shelter, and clean water.

Hospitals also provide much-needed assistance after storms. Firefighters, police, and trained rescue dogs look for injured survivors and provide the much-needed basic services that keep citizens alive and help communities get back on their feet. Disaster response and relief are becoming ever more important to communities and governments as killer storms and weather-related disasters increase due to global warming.

# CHAPTER four

## What Comes Next?

As a nation, and as members of the international community, we have a lot of work to do to help slow and eventually reverse the effects of climate change. Severe storms are a serious side effect of climate change, one that threatens businesses, property, homes, and human lives. In some ways, we are still in the early stages of learning about climate change. Scientists are constantly coming out with new research and information that can help shape what we know about the links between weather, human activity, climate, and climate change.

# SPACE-BASED RESEARCH

Research is the key to future learning. In October of 2010, the National Aeronautics and Space Administration (NASA) and the U.S. Agency for International Development (USAID) unveiled a global climate change research system. It is an environmental imaging and management system that

The Soil Moisture and Ocean Salinity Earth Explorer satellite collects data that can be used to study global surface temperatures.

uses satellite images to collect data. Analysis of this data helps distinguish between short-term variations in weather and longer-term shifts in climate. This not only helps clarify the extent to which Earth is warming and its climate changing, but also results in more accurate and detailed weather forecasts. The data can also be used to craft better disaster response strategies, policies, and procedures.

There is also new technology being developed in Europe to further the study of climate change. The European Space Agency launched a satellite into space in February of 2010. The Soil Moisture and Ocean Salinity (SMOS) satellite maps the amount of water in the soil and the salinity of the

# ENGINEERING THE FUTURE

When scientists and engineers try to make safer homes, they simulate storm conditions to test new building materials. They use storm simulations and wind tunnels featuring sustained gusts of over 165 miles per hour (266 km/hr). They also simulate the effect flying debris has upon structures, including siding, exterior walls, and windows. Based on their research, scientists decide which building materials are strongest and most likely to weather intense storms with a minimum of damage. They study even the smallest variables, such as in which direction a door or window should open in order to make the building as strong as possible in even the most adverse conditions.

ocean. These are key factors that are affected by increasing global surface temperatures. Greater levels of water in the soil would indicate increased precipitation and flooding, while lower ocean salinity points to increased melting of glaciers. The satellite makes global maps of the soil and ocean every three days with great accuracy. Some scientists suspect that the rate of climate change is different over land than it is over the ocean, so SMOS data will test this hypothesis and refine climate models.

## STORM-PROOFING

When buildings are constructed in tornado, hurricane, blizzard, or flood zones, special precautions are taken to make those homes and businesses as strong as possible. An EF 5 tornado on the Fujita Tornado Scale, a Category 5 hurricane on the Saffir-Simpson Hurricane Scale, or a river that has overflowed its banks can be a dangerous and even deadly event for the people in the area. After tornadoes repeatedly ravaged the central United States in the spring of 2011, new legislation in Oklahoma required more rigorous building codes so that buildings could withstand more intense storm activity—up to the strength of an EF-5 tornado. Buildings would also be required to have storm shelters for the added protection of their occupants.

In the future, these kinds of destructive storms will likely be more widespread. Tornadoes will occur more frequently, and not only in Tornado Alley. Hurricanes will not only hit areas closest to the tropics. This means that building codes

A family tries to salvage their belongings after a tornado ripped through their home in Joplin, Missouri.

nationwide will need to be reviewed and revised in order to ensure that buildings are able to withstand various kinds of killer storms. Areas that were once hit with only hurricanes in the summer can also be hit with tornadoes in the spring or even blizzards in winter. The problem is that, realistically, not all older homes are going to be retrofitted with the latest storm-safety enhancements and technologies. The cost for most homeowners would be too great. While future homes will likely feature the latest storm-proofing features and technology, older homes will likely remain highly vulnerable to the destructive effects of intense storms.

In an attempt to address the high costs of retrofitting older homes and buildings, local, state, and federal governments are beginning to offer incentives to residents of storm-prone areas to storm-proof their homes. These incentives take the form of tax credits, sales-tax holidays, and government grants. These home and building improvements will keep citizens safer, and they will cut down on insurance costs. In 2010, property damage caused by storms totaled over $20 billion. Just about $13 billion of that was covered by insurance, which means that many home and business owners were left with significant financial losses due to the storms. Damage losses were up 30 percent from the year before, and the numbers keep rising each year.

# CHAPTER five

## Taking Action Today

When the future brings the promise of more frequent and intense storms, humans must learn to survive in changing and dangerous conditions. Tackling the problem will require everyone's help. Laws and policies must be changed at the local, state, and federal levels of government to address climate change and reduce carbon-based emissions. In addition, all citizens must commit themselves to lifestyle and consumer choices that will reduce their individual and collective carbon footprints.

Get to know a political leader's position on climate change. Support those politicians who are actively committed to reducing carbon emissions and developing alternative energy sources. These are important ways for ordinary citizens to influence government policy and action on the environment. When a politician feels that a given topic is important to voters, more attention will be paid to it. It will become more likely that policies will be made to limit greenhouse gas emissions. More money may be given to develop new energy technologies that do not rely on the burning of fossil fuels. In this way, ordinary people have the power to influence policy making and policy makers.

## TAKING ACTION ON THE LOCAL LEVEL

On the local level, you can be most helpful by providing help to your community after damaging weather events. Find out how to donate to or volunteer for a local chapter of the American Red Cross or other nonprofit or charity organizations that help those in need. It is a great way to provide help for your neighbors after an emergency. After a storm, communities and towns may be left without electricity or clean water. They need donations from the community to help them get back on their feet. Organizations sometimes take contributions of food, water, clean clothing, toiletries, or anything else that can be spared for people who are trying to get back on their feet and rebuild their lives.

Volunteering to help clean up after severe weather events is an excellent way to get involved and make a difference. Make sure you sign up with a responsible adult who can

Volunteers for the American Red Cross help citizens seeking shelter from flooding after Tropical Storm Irene hit their upstate New York town.

work alongside you and keep you safe while helping out in possibly hazardous conditions. Local scouting and student volunteer groups can also work together to assist and clean up a storm-ravaged community. Checking local newspaper listings is a good way to find out about some of these community-minded organizations.

## TAKING ACTION ON THE STATE LEVEL

At the state level, you can get involved with groups that promote environmental protection and awareness, lobby state lawmakers, and influence state policy. Just as each nation can pledge to reduce its carbon output by a certain amount each year, so can states. Citizens' opinions and actions regarding carbon emissions and environmental protection have a definite influence on representatives in state government.

It is a politician's job to listen to and thoughtfully consider the requests and opinions of a state's citizens. If citizens speak in large enough numbers, representatives are more likely to hear and act upon their requests. So get friends, family, and like-minded local organizations together and make a joint effort. Many voices delivering the same message at once are heard more clearly and powerfully than just one voice or many scattered and ill-coordinated ones.

Let officials know that you no longer want your state's industries, offices, utilities, companies, factories, and homes relying exclusively upon the burning of fossil fuels to generate their energy. Press your state politicians to monitor and make public relevant data concerning the state's carbon emissions. Offer practical suggestions about alternative energy sources, such as solar and wind power. Support any decisions your government makes that are environmentally responsible, and reward the politicians that champion them with your vote (or, if you are not yet of voting age, volunteer for their campaigns and encourage your parents and other adult family members to vote for them). Make it clear that you support these efforts and would like to see similar decisions made in the future.

# TAKING ACTION ON THE FEDERAL LEVEL

When supporting and choosing a national leader, it is important to know his or her stand on environmental issues. A president's or congressperson's environmental philosophy will have an enormous impact upon federal policies and laws, both during and potentially far beyond his or her time in office.

Many people enter the voting booth without being aware of a candidate's position on important environmental issues. At this point in history, with global warming a widely accepted phenomenon, with climate change well underway, and with its ripple effects—such as more frequent and intense storms—spreading worldwide, this is not the time to remain ignorant of or overlook a candidate's environmental track record or philosophy. Consult with leading environmental groups to determine how well they grade the candidate before supporting, volunteering for, or voting for that person.

# CHOOSING ALTERNATIVE ENERGY SOURCES

Apart from political action, citizens can do a lot individually and collectively to cut down on the output of greenhouse gases. Ordinary people do not have to wait for government or industry to take the lead; they can take effective action immediately by choosing energy sources that do not rely on burning fossil fuels. When we pollute less, we help protect and heal the environment. When we use solar- or

Alternative sources of energy, such as solar power, reduce the amount of greenhouse gases being released into the atmosphere.

wind-powered energy methods, we are not putting heat-trapping greenhouse gases into the atmosphere.

Taking care not to waste energy is also a good way to help the environment and reduce carbon emissions. Today's world population is about seven billion people. Just fifty years ago, it was three billion. In 1900, it was just 1.6 billion. As the world's population has exploded, so, too, has its energy needs and reliance on fossil fuels. This increase

Wind power is another alternative energy source that reduces greenhouse gas emissions and can help combat global warming. Unlike carbon-based fuel, wind power and solar power are clean and renewable resources.

in population and energy consumption only contributes to a warming atmosphere and related climate change. If billions of humans are going to be able to continue living on this planet, with adequate food and water supplies and a climate that fosters life, they are going to have to embrace clean alternative energy sources. They must also radically reduce the amount of greenhouse gases emitted into and collecting in the atmosphere.

# LISTENING TO WARNINGS

Just as animals and plants can successfully adapt to changes in their ecosystems, humans must attempt to find a way to survive in the midst of increasing storm activity and ferocity. We know that animals seek shelter and build homes that they know are safe from the elements. Humans must do the same, employing new building policies, strategies, techniques, materials, and technologies to best protect the lives contained within storm-battered structures.

When storm warnings are issued, the smartest thing for people to do is listen to and heed those warnings. They are meant to save lives and property, even if they require inconvenient responses, such as mandatory evacuation. Even though evacuations are inconvenient, they save lives. The decision to call for an evacuation is not made lightly. It is done with great consideration for the safety of the community and an awareness of how dislocating the process can be for residents and business owners. It is important for people to heed evacuation warnings and not try to "ride out" a looming storm. People who choose to stay behind during storms may be risking the lives of first responders who could be sent in after them if trouble arises. If people heed the warnings and alerts issued by the authorities, lives can be saved and injuries can be avoided.

Animals instinctively seek safe shelter in times of danger, but humans sometimes feel that they are invincible. They feel that the buildings around them are strong enough

# MAKING A DIFFERENCE

April 2011 was a record-breaking month in terms of the amount of tornadoes that tore through Tornado Alley in the American Midwest. Affected communities required lots of outside assistance to cope with and clean up the destruction left in the killer storms' wakes. Helping those in need is one of the most important ways that we can adapt to the changing climate and the increased storminess it spawns.

A group of fifty-five students from a high school in southwest Virginia decided to spend their spring break helping those in need after a tornado hit a northwestern Ohio town. They worked with a national relief network to clear debris and cut up trees that had fallen on people's properties. Their effort was greatly appreciated by those who needed a little extra help during a difficult time. The sooner communities can get back on their feet after devastating storms, the better they will be able to adapt to storms that strike in the future.

to survive against the worst that nature can throw at them. They doubt the accuracy of forecasts or suspect media hype is behind dire warnings. They feel that the odds that they will be injured or killed are low and not worth the inconvenience of evacuating and moving to a secure public shelter or to the homes of friends or family members outside the danger zone. Many people feel the need to remain in and guard their homes while a killer storm is passing through. But the winds of even a Category 1 hurricane or an even weaker tropical storm can still cause tremendous death and destruction.

First responders have a difficult job rescuing people from storms. Instead of being with their own families or protecting their own homes, they are out in dangerous conditions rescuing people who are facing life-threatening situations. People who fail to leave when an evacuation order is issued often end up putting not only themselves in mortal danger, but also the first responders who attempt to save them. This is why it is important to heed all storm-related warnings when they are given. You are not only keeping yourself safe, you are keeping others safe as well. That way, first responders can concentrate on the job of emergency management and cleanup and get the community back on its feet faster.

## TOWARD THE FUTURE, TOGETHER

Storms that are both more frequent and more intense are a likely future reality. It is only by thinking and acting as a community—a community of local townspeople, state residents, countrymen and women, and global citizens—that we will successfully adapt to climate change and hopefully begin to reverse its worst effects. The days of selfish, individualistic action and wasteful and careless consumption are over. We must all come together and share the sacrifices and work as a global community of brothers and sisters. We must all join forces to secure our planet—the only home and shelter we humans have—against the ravages of past human activity. And we must turn our gaze toward tomorrow and change our habits and practices in order to guarantee a place for human life in the planet's future.

carbon dioxide  A greenhouse gas naturally present in the air, but also produced by the burning of fossil fuels.

climate change  A long-term change in Earth's climate, usually seen as a result of human activity; a consequence of global warming.

climate model  A computer model that predicts future climate conditions over a specific period of time.

cyclone  A tropical storm or hurricane that forms in the Southern Hemisphere.

Fujita Tornado Scale  A rating scale that categorizes the strength of tornado winds on a scale of 0 to 6, with 6 being the strongest.

Global Change Research Act  A U.S. law passed in 1990 that requires research into global warming and related issues, such as climate change and the environmental, economic, health, and safety consequences of climate change.

global warming  A significant and sustained increase in global surface and ocean temperatures; a consequence of human activity (such as the burning of fossil fuels) and the buildup of heat-trapping carbon emissions and other greenhouse gases in the atmosphere.

greenhouse effect  The trapping of the sun's warmth in Earth's lower atmosphere.

greenhouse gases  Gases that contribute to the greenhouse effect, such as carbon dioxide and methane.

hurricane  A storm that forms over the ocean with wind speeds over 74 miles per hour (119 km/hr).

Saffir-Simpson Hurricane Scale  A rating scale that categorizes hurricane wind strength on a scale of 1 to 5, with 5 being the strongest.

tropical storm  A storm that forms over the ocean with winds of at least 39 miles per hour (63 km/hr).

typhoon  A tropical storm or hurricane that forms in the Indian or Western Pacific Ocean.

Canadian International Development Agency (CIDA)
200 Promenade du Portage
Gatineau, QC C1A 0G4
Canada
(800) 230-6349
Web site: http://www.acdi-cida.gc.ca
The CIDA is Canada's leading agency for international
assistance and aid, including for victims of weather
disasters, flooding, and drought.

Cities for Climate Protection
15 Shattuck Square, Suite 215
Berkeley, CA 94704
(510) 540-8843
Web site: http://www.iclei.org/co2
Cities for Climate Protection promotes reductions in green-
house gas emissions in towns and cities across the
United States.

Climate Action Network Canada
412-1 Nicholas Street
Ottawa, ON K1N 7B7
Canada
(613) 241-4413
Web site: http://www.climateactionnetwork.ca
Climate Action Network Canada is an organization of members committed to preventing human interference in the
global climate. It also promotes renewable energy as a
method of reducing greenhouse gas emissions.

Federal Emergency Management Agency (FEMA)
P.O. Box 10055

Hyattsville, MD 20782-8055
(800) 827-8112
Web site: http://www.fema.gov
FEMA is a division of the U.S. Department of Homeland
    Security and supports first responders and citizens who
    have been endangered by disasters such as severe
    weather events.

Friends of the Earth
1717 Massachusetts Avenue, Suite 600
Washington, DC 20036
(202) 783-7400
Web site: http://www.foe.org
Friends of the Earth and its network of grassroots groups in
    seventy-seven countries defend the environment and
    champion a more healthy and just world. Its current
    campaigns focus on clean energy and solutions to
    global warming; protecting people from toxic and new,
    potentially harmful technologies; and promoting smarter,
    low-pollution transportation alternatives.

National Oceanic and Atmospheric Administration (NOAA)
1401 Constitution Avenue NW, Room 5128
Washington, DC 20230
(301) 713-1208
Web site: http://www.noaa.gov
The NOAA is a U.S. agency that studies the atmosphere and
    oceans. Its mission is to understand and predict environ-
    mental changes so that we can make the best use of our
    resources. One of its divisions is the National Weather
    Service. Its Web site has tools and information on practically
    all aspects of climate science and lots of student resources.

Nature Conservancy
4245 North Fairfax Drive, Suite 100
Arlington, VA 22203-1606
(703) 841-5300
Web site: http://www.nature.org
This conservation organization has ongoing projects around
   the world aimed at the protection of land and water. It
   identifies principal threats to marine life, freshwater
   ecosystems, forests, and protected areas, then uses a
   scientific approach to save them.

Pew Center on Global Climate Change
2101 Wilson Boulevard, Suite 550
Arlington, VA 22201
(703) 516-4146
Web site: http://www.pewclimate.org
The Pew Center on Global Climate Change works to
   develop solutions to climate change.

Sierra Club
85 Second Street, 2nd Floor
San Francisco, CA 94105
(415) 977-5500
Web site: http://www.sierraclub.org
One of America's biggest environmental protection groups
   has programs for volunteers to get involved in protecting
   water supplies and other resources. Its Web site has
   resources for students and links to local chapters across
   the United States.

Union of Concerned Scientists
2 Brattle Square

Cambridge, MA 02238-9105
(617) 547 5552
Web site: http://www.ucsusa.org
The Union of Concerned Scientists works to educate the
    public about issues relating to climate change.

U.S. Global Change Research Program
1717 Pennsylvania Avenue NW, Suite 250
Washington, DC 20006
(202) 223-6262
Web site: http://www.globalchange.gov
Begun in 1989, the U.S. Global Change Research
    Program coordinates and integrates federal research
    on changes in the global environment and their impli-
    cations for society. The program engages in activities
    aimed at strengthening climate change research in the
    United States.

# WEB SITES

Due to the changing nature of Internet links, Rosen
Publishing has developed an online list of Web sites related
to the subject of this book. This site is updated regularly.
Please use this link to access the list:

http://www.rosenlinks.com/sttr/storm

# FOR FURTHER READing

Bailey, Gerry. *Changing Climate*. New York, NY: Gareth Stevens Publishing, 2011.

Benoit, Peter. *Climate Change: A True Book*. New York, NY: Scholastic Library Publishing, 2011.

Bradman, Tony. *Under the Weather: Stories About Climate Change*. London, England: Frances Lincoln Children's Books, 2010.

Carson, Mary Kay. *Inside Weather*. New York, NY: Sterling Publishing, 2011.

Eyewitness Books. *Climate Change: Eyewitness Guide*. New York, NY: Dorling Kindersley, 2011.

Hynes, Margaret. *Extreme Weather*. New York, NY: Kingfisher, 2011.

Levete, Sarah. *Catastrophic Weather*. New York, NY: Crabtree Publishing Co., 2010.

Marcovitz, Hal. *How Serious a Threat Is Climate Change?* San Diego, CA: ReferencePoint Press, 2011.

Ollhoff, Jim. *Climate Change: Living in a Warmer World*. Edina, MN: ABDO Publishing Co., 2010.

Ollhoff, Jim. *Climate Change: Myths and Controversies*. Edina, MN: ABDO Publishing Co., 2010.

Oxlade, Chris. *Climate Change*. Mankato, MN: Black Rabbit Books, 2010.

Parker, Janice. *Weather: Science Q & A*. New York, NY: Weigl Publishers, 2008.

Rafferty, John P. *Climate and Climate Change*. New York, NY: Britannica Educational Publishing, 2011.

Solway, Andrew. *Climate Change*. Mankato, MN: Black Rabbit Books, 2010.

Spilsbury, Richard. *Ask an Expert: Climate Change*. New York, NY: Crabtree Publishing Co., 2010.

Ahrens, C. Donald, and Perry J. Samson. *Extreme Weather and Climate*. Belmont, CA: Brooks/Cole, 2010.

Biello, David. "Can Climate Models Predict Global Warming's Direct Effect on Your City?" *Scientific American*, March 23, 2010. Retrieved September 2011 (http://www.scientificamerican.com/article.cfm?id= climate-models-predict-global-warming-effects-in-cities).

Broder, John M. "Climate-Change Debate Is Heating Up in Deep Freeze." *New York Times*, February 10, 2010. Retrieved September 2011 (http://www.nytimes.com/ 2010/02/11/science/earth/11climate.html).

Bucco, Gloria. "Flood of the Century: Remembering the Great Midwest Flood of 1993." Nebraska Department of Natural Resources. Retrieved September 2011. (http://dnr.ne.gov/ floodplain/PDF_Files/FloodUpdateStory_Rev3.pdf).

Burt, Christopher C. *Extreme Weather: A Guide and Record Book*. New York, NY: W. W. Norton & Co., 2007.

Congressional Budget Office. *Potential Impacts of Climate Change in the United States*. Washington, DC: Congressional Budget Office, 2009.

Cullen, Heidi. *The Weather of the Future: Heat Waves, Extreme Storms, and Other Scenes from a Climate-Changed Planet*. New York, NY: Harper, 2010.

Eilperin, Juliet. "U.S. Pledges 17 Percent Emissions Reduction by 2020." *Washington Post*, January 29, 2010. Retrieved September 2011 (http://www .washingtonpost.com/wp-dyn/content/article/2010/ 01/28/AR2010012803632.html).

European Space Agency. "Mapping Soil Moisture and Ocean Salinity." Retrieved September 2011 (http://www .esa.int/esaMI/smos/SEMSKJ6CTWF_0.html).

Gore, Al. *Our Choice: A Plan to Solve the Climate Crisis*. Emmaus, PA: Rodale, 2009.

Grant, Kelli B. "New Incentives to Storm-Proof Homes." *Wall Street Journal*, May 17, 2011. Retrieved September 2011 (http://blogs.wsj.com/developments/2011/05/17/new-incentives-to-storm-proof-homes).

Hoggan, James. *Climate Cover-Up: The Crusade to Deny Global Warming*. Vancouver, BC, Canada: Greystone Books, 2009.

Hollingshead, Mike, and Eric Nguyen. *Adventures in Tornado Alley: The Storm Chasers*. London, England: Thames & Hudson, 2008.

Kahl, Jonathan D. W. *National Audubon Society First Field Guide: Weather*. New York, NY: Scholastic Reference, 1998.

Mogil, R. Michael. *Extreme Weather: Understanding the Science of Hurricanes, Tornadoes, Floods, Heat Waves, Snow Storms, Global Warming, and Other Atmospheric Disturbances*. New York, NY: Black Dog & Leventhal Publishers, 2007.

Murphy, Barb. "Cutting Edge Technology to Combat Climate Change." National Academies Press. Retrieved September 4, 2011 (http://notes.nap.edu/2010/11/02/cutting-edge-technology-to-combat-climate-change).

National Oceanic and Atmospheric Administration. "2011 Tornado Information." Retrieved September 2011 (http://www.noaanews.noaa.gov/2011_tornado_information.html).

National Weather Service. "The Saffir-Simpson Hurricane Wind Scale." Retrieved September 2011 (http://www.nhc.noaa.gov/sshws.shtml).

National Weather Service Weather Forecast Office. "The Great Flood of 1993." Retrieved September 2011 (http://www.crh.noaa.gov/dvn/?n=071993_greatflood).

Preston, Ray. "ER Doctor Gives First-Hand Account of the Joplin Tornado." KMOV.com, May 27, 2011. Retrieved September 2011 (http://www.kmov.com/news/local/A-First-Hand-Account-of-the-Joplin-Tornado-122725184.html).

Sala de Premsa. "SMOS: Cutting-Edge Technology for Monitoring Climate Change." Universitat Politència de Catalunya, February 15, 2010. Retrieved September 2011 (http://www.upc.edu/saladepremsa/informacio/monografics/smos-cutting-edge-technology-for-monitoring).

Schneider, Bonnie. *Extreme Weather: A Guide to Surviving Flash Floods, Tornadoes, Hurricanes, Heat Waves, Snowstorms, Tsunamis, and Other Natural Disasters*. New York, NY: Palgrave Macmillan, 2012.

Science Daily. "Global Warming Causes Severe Storms." Retrieved September 2001 (http://www.sciencedaily.com/videos/2009/0109-global_warming_causes_severe_storms.htm).

Semple, Kirk. "On Flood Plain, Pondering Wisdom of Rebuilding Anew." *New York Times*, September 4, 2011. Retrieved September 2011 (http://www.nytimes.com/2011/09/05/nyregion/for-a-town-on-a-flood-plain-doubts-about-rebuilding.html?_r=1&pagewanted=all).

Timmer, Reed. *Into the Storm: Violent Tornadoes, Killer Hurricanes, and Death-Defying Adventures in Extreme Weather*. New York, NY: Dutton Adult, 2010.

Ward, Peter Douglas. *The Flooded Earth: Our Future in a World Without Ice Caps*. New York, NY: Basic Books, 2010.

# INDex

## ABOUT THE AUTHOR

Adam Furgang has written several books about the environment, including a book about green transportation and reducing your carbon footprint. He loves photographing intense weather events, especially lightning storms. He lives in upstate New York with his wife and two sons.

## PHOTO CREDITS